Life Stories
Anne Frank

Wayne Jackman

Illustrated by Jon Davis

D1103346

Wayland

Life Stories

Louis Braille
Christopher Columbus
Anne Frank
Gandhi
Helen Keller
Martin Luther King
Florence Nightingale
Mother Teresa

Cover and frontispiece: *Anne Frank, aged thirteen, in 1942 – the year her family went into hiding.*

Series editor: Anna Girling
Consultant: Nigel Smith
Designer: Loraine Hayes

This edition published in 1998 by
Wayland (Publishers) Ltd

First published in 1992 by
Wayland (Publishers) Ltd
61 Western Road, Hove
East Sussex, BN3 1JD, England

British Library Cataloguing in Publication Data
Jackman, Wayne
Anne Frank.—(Life Stories Series)
I. Title   II. Davis, Jon   III. Series
940.531503924

PAPERBACK ISBN 0-7502-1677-8

Typeset by Dorchester Typesetting Group Ltd
Printed in Italy by G. Canale & C.S.p.A., Turin

Contents

Words printed in **bold** appear in the glossary.

Early childhood in Germany

Anne Frank was born on 12 June 1929 in Frankfurt, Germany. She came from a Jewish family who had lived there for hundreds of years. Anne's parents were called Otto and Edith. Her father worked in a bank. The Franks' three-year-old daughter, Margot, was very pleased when Anne was born. She was glad to have a little sister to play with.

Anne's father was a very keen photographer. He took dozens of photos of Anne and Margot as they played in the street or visited their grandparents.

In Germany Jewish people were sometimes treated very unfairly. This is called **anti-Semitism**. But in Frankfurt, anti-Semitism was not as bad as in other parts of Germany. Although Anne's family was not rich, her life was happy and fun.

Anne with her father and sister, Margot (left).

5

Hitler comes to power

In 1933, when Anne was four, **Hitler** became leader of Germany. His followers were called **Nazis**. Hitler believed that the German people were the best and strongest race in the world. He called them **Aryans**. He thought all other races of people, especially the Jewish people, were **inferior** to the Aryans.

Hitler began to pass unfair laws against black people, gypsies and Jews. He put many of these people into special prisons called **concentration camps**. A great number of them died in the camps.

Hitler at a rally. He had many Nazi supporters in Germany.

The Nazi symbol was a swastika – the bent cross on the men's armbands.

Hitler told Germans not to buy anything from Jewish shopkeepers, and Jews were not allowed to work for the government. Anne could not go to nursery school because she was a 'non-Aryan'. Otto Frank saw that things were getting bad for Jews, so he moved his family to Amsterdam in the Netherlands.

Settling in the Netherlands

Anne and Margot led a happy life in the Netherlands.

Anne and her family started a new life in Amsterdam. They quickly learnt to speak Dutch, and Otto Frank started a business selling pectine (used to make jams and marmalade). Anne's grandmother came from Germany to live with the family.

The Franks made many friends among other Jewish **refugees** and the local Dutch people. The family went on many outings.

Anne aged six. She was very fond of music and reading.

Anne (right) was popular and made many friends in Amsterdam.

Anne and Margot did well at school, although Anne was often scolded by her teachers for being a chatterbox. Anne was very popular at school — especially with the boys, who often asked if they could cycle home with her. After school she liked playing ping-pong and meeting friends at ice-cream parlours.

At home, Anne's parents encouraged her to play and listen to music, and the family often gathered together to read out loud to each other. Reading was one of Anne's favourite pastimes and, like her father, she was very fond of Greek and Roman stories.

Anne was able to live a normal, busy life just like any other young girl. But this was soon to change.

The invasion of the Netherlands

In 1940, eight months after the start of the **Second World War**, Hitler ordered the German army to invade the Netherlands. For the 140,000 Jews in the Netherlands, life would never be the same again.

Otto Frank tried to get his family out of the country. Like many other Jews, he was unable to leave, so Anne and her family again had to face up to life under Nazi rule.

The Nazi Germans invaded the Netherlands. Many Jews tried to escape.

The Nazis ruled that all Jews had to wear yellow stars on their clothes.

Hitler introduced the same unfair laws in the Netherlands as he had in Germany. Dutch Jews had to wear a yellow star on their clothes to show they were Jews. They were not allowed to visit theatres or cinemas. They had to buy their food from special 'Jewish' shops. They could not ride on trams or be out after eight o'clock in the evening.

Even with all these unfair rules, Anne wrote that her life 'was still bearable. Life goes on in spite of all'. Otto Frank was not so sure. He began planning a secret hiding place.

Going into hiding

In 1942, two years after the Germans invaded, Anne's grandmother died. Anne was very sad, but her thirteenth birthday cheered her up. Anne's favourite present was a wonderful notebook, which she decided to use as a diary. Anne's diary was to become her best friend, and she called it Kitty.

Only three weeks later the family received a bad shock. Margot was ordered to report for work at a German **labour camp**. The Franks knew what this meant. Margot, because she was Jewish, would be sent to a concentration camp where she would almost certainly be killed.

The office building where Anne's father worked, as it is today.

Many Jews were put to death by poisonous gas in concentration camps. Today, we call these terrible killings **the Holocaust**.

That night Otto Frank decided that the whole family must hide away in the secret place he had been preparing for months. They could take only a few things with them because they might have been stopped by the police if they carried

suitcases. Anne took her hair curlers, school books, some old letters, a comb and, of course, her diary. She knew they were crazy things to take, but she said, 'I'm not sorry; memories mean more to me than dresses.'

Left *The Franks hid in secret rooms at the back of the office building.*

Hiding in the annexe

Otto Frank took his family to some rooms at the top of the building where he had his office. This part of the building was known as 'the **annexe**'. It was at the back of the building and was hidden from view.

Anne helped to scrub the rooms clean. To brighten up her room, she pinned pictures of film stars on the walls.

A few Dutch friends who worked for Otto Frank agreed to bring food each day, and one of them built a movable bookcase to hide the door to the annexe. Anne and her family hoped the Germans would never find them.

Anne decorated her room with pictures of film stars.

The secret door to the annexe was hidden behind a bookcase. The pictures show it closed (left) and open (right).

Soon another four Jews came to share the hiding place; among them was a teenage boy named Peter Van Daan. At first Anne thought Peter was silly, but eventually they became good friends.

With eight people now hiding in the annexe, life was very difficult. Often there was not enough food to go round, and Anne had to eat rotten vegetables. The beds had to be lifted up and put away each morning because there was not enough space. During the day everyone had to keep completely silent. Any noise could give away their hiding place to the people working in another part of the building, who might tell the Germans.

Anne wrote in her diary every day.

Anne continued to write in Kitty, her diary, every day. She wrote down all her thoughts and all about her life in hiding. She was a natural writer, and she realized that more than anything she wanted to be a writer when the war was over.

Anne's diary became her best friend; she told Kitty all her secrets.

Life in hiding was not always gloomy. Birthdays were celebrated, and presents exchanged. Anne used to make sweets and practise her ballet steps.

On 6 June 1944, after nearly two years in hiding, everyone in the annexe was overjoyed to hear on the secret radio that the **Allied armies** of Britain and the USA had landed in France. Surely now the war would soon be over and they would all be free.

Soldiers from the Allied armies freed the Netherlands. But it was too late to save Anne's family.

Capture

Two months later, on 4 August, everyone hiding in the annexe heard the sound they had all dreaded. A loud knock on the door and a German voice shouting, 'Open up. Gestapo.' The Gestapo were the German secret police. Someone had **betrayed** their hiding place! No one ever found out who it was.

One of the policemen took Otto Frank's briefcase. Everything in it, including Anne's diary, was thrown on the floor.

The eight people who had hidden for so long were arrested. Later they were put on the last train ever to carry Jews to the concentration camps.

In the concentration camps conditions were terrible. Edith Frank died of starvation. Anne and Margot were then sent to another camp where they both caught **typhus**. When Margot died, Anne's spirit was finally broken. She died a few days later.

Conditions in the concentration camps were terrible. It was very difficult to keep clean.

The diary is published

Otto Frank was the only member of his family to survive the war. He returned to Amsterdam hoping Anne might still be alive. There he learnt that she had died. One of the Dutch friends who used to bring food to the hiding place in the annexe had found Anne's diary on the floor and kept it safe. She gave it to Otto Frank and persuaded him to publish it as a book.

The diary was published in 1947. It caught the imagination of the whole world. Anne's talent for writing and the tragedy of her short life seemed to say everything about the terrible war and the hateful Nazis.

Today, *The Diary of Anne Frank* has been translated into dozens of languages and more than 20 million copies have been sold. It has been made into a stage play, a film and a ballet.

Anne wrote, 'I want to go on living after my death. And therefore I am grateful to God for giving me this gift of expressing all that is in me.' Anne certainly has lived on after her death. Her diary is a reminder of the suffering caused when people treat others unfairly just because of their race, religion or the colour of their skin.

Date chart

1929 Anne Frank born on 12 June in Frankfurt, Germany.

1933 Hitler comes to power in Germany.

1933 Anne Frank's family moves to Amsterdam in the Netherlands.

1939 Second World War begins.

1940 The German army invades and occupies the Netherlands.

1940 Anne Frank's family tries and fails to move to England.

1941 Many unfair laws passed against Jewish people in the Netherlands.

1942 Anne is given a diary as a present on her thirteenth birthday. Anne and her family go into hiding in the secret annexe.

1944 6 June. The Allied armies land in France and begin the liberation of countries occupied by the Germans.

1944 4 August. Someone reveals the Franks' hiding place. All the people living in the annexe are arrested and sent away to concentration camps.

1945 March. Anne Frank and her sister Margot die of typhus in Belsen camp.

1945 8 May. The German army surrenders. The war is over.

1947 Anne Frank's diary is published. More than 20 million copies have been sold.

Glossary

Allied armies The armies from forty-nine countries that fought against Hitler and the Nazis during the Second World War.

Annexe A building attached to a larger building.

Anti-Semitism Treating Jewish people unfairly, just because they are Jewish.

Aryan A race of people believed by the Nazis to be the best in the world. Aryans were non-Jewish Europeans.

Betray To reveal or give up a person to an enemy.

Concentration camps Special prisons set up by the Nazis for certain types of people that Hitler thought were inferior, such as Jews, gypsies and blacks. Many people died in concentration camps.

Hitler The leader of Germany from 1933 to 1945 and head of the Nazi party. Hitler blamed Germany's problems on the Jews, and he tried to get rid of all Jews in Europe.

The Holocaust The mass murder of the Jews by the Nazis during the Second World War. About six million Jews were killed.

Inferior Of less worth.

Labour camp A place where prisoners had to work for the Nazis.

Nazis Members of Adolf Hitler's National Socialist German Workers' Party.

Refugees People who move from their own country to seek safety in another country.

Second World War The fighting that broke out in many parts of the world between 1939 and 1945. It started when Germany invaded Poland and involved many countries.

Typhus A serious illness caused by a poor diet and filthy conditions.

Books to read

For older readers:

Anne Frank Journal (Anne Frank Foundation, Amsterdam, 1988)

The Diary of Anne Frank by Anne Frank (Pan Books, 1982)

Eva's Story (A Step-sister's Story) by Eva Schloss (W. H. Allen, 1988)

Tales from the House Behind by Anne Frank (Piccolo, 1971)

For younger readers:

Anne Frank by Angela Bull (Hamish Hamilton, 1984)

Anne Frank by Vanora Leigh (Wayland, 1985)

Anne Frank by Richard Tames (Franklin Watts, 1989)

For further information:
The Anne Frank Trust,
43 Portland Place,
London W1.
Tel: 071 323 0696

Index

Picture acknowledgements
The publishers would like to thank the
following for allowing their pictures to
be reproduced in this book: Anne
Frank Stichting (Anne Frank
Foundation), Amsterdam 5, 8, 9, 10,
16, 17, 18, 19, 20; Popperfoto 26;
Topham 6, 7, 13, 23; Wayland Picture
Library 14.